The
Money Metrics
MANUAL

It's Your Money

Keep More Of It

By

Robert Pessemier

Second Edition

Compliments of:

www.Money-Metrics.com

Phone: 425-373-4045

Table of Contents

More information also at www.Money-Metrics.com or 425-373-4045.

Note: This manual is designed to provide information and ideas on the subject matter covered. The author is not engaged in rendering legal, accounting, or other regulated professional services.

Feel like you work harder, save less, and borrow more? Most people do. Did you know that a 14% credit card is effectively a 91% loan? Most people don't. It is my hope that this manual will have a profound impact on your financial future.

As a Licensed Mortgage Broker and Accredited Asset Management Specialist I talk with people every day about their financial situation. Some people are in great shape. No debt, no issues, no worries. They are few in number. Most people feel some measure of financial stress. They are looking for a better way to handle money. This guide should help.

The Results

People who have followed these guidelines:

- Feel like they have been given a raise!

- Have renewed hope in their financial future. They know they can and will change their lives for the better.

- Have a plan for spending their money.

- Have an emergency fund for when "life" happens.

- Have no debt and can invest in their future.

- Make choices in life rather than just react to it.

When I was in the Fire Service my job was to help people. Sometimes we had to go put out a raging fire, sometimes we would teach people about fire prevention. Now I am a financial firefighter. Some people are in the middle of a financial house fire, some people just smell a little smoke, and some just need a little education. I use different tools, and solve different problems, but the goal is the same. I hope you will also experience positive results from this information.

More information also at www.Money-Metrics.com or 425-373-4045.

For Employers

The biggest stress employees face at work is from their personal financial situation. Research has shown that personal financial education has a 300% return for the employer. Increased productivity, better use of company funds and expenses, reduced absenteeism; increased morale and other benefits come to companies who help employees learn to handle money better. It is my hope that you will be a company that will participate in the educational process. They're your profits. Have more of them.

We have done a little estimating and here is what we found. If we can add an average of just 5 minutes per day of productive time to your bottom line, you will save or gain $1,000 per year per employee. So how many employees do you have? Average employee personal savings is over $3,300 per year. They're your biggest assets; help them hang on to more of their money. Who knows, they might even thank you for it!

Money Metrics

> "It's what you learn after you know it all that counts."
>
> John Wooden

Do you find yourself working harder, saving less, and borrowing more just to make ends meet? Is your credit card debt getting a little high? House payment feeling uncomfortable? Money comes and goes and none of it seems to stick around. The usual pattern is goes like this: get paid; pay the bills; spend what's left.

In 40 years of working at an average income of $50,000 per year, 2 million dollars will pass through your hands. It's not how much money you <u>make</u>, but how much you <u>keep</u> that matters. How much will be used to forward your goals and dreams, and how much will be wasted on credit card debt or taken by other money grabbers.

Whether you make a lot, or just a little, it's frustrating when you can't manage money as well as you would like. Most of us never learned how. This book will help.

We don't change what we don't measure and understand. We need to understand the basic metrics of money management that will help us make good financial decisions. This handbook provides that education and will help you manage money better. It will guide you through the fundamental skills and concepts so that you can gain control and achieve real financial results.

Most people are on the wrong side of the money trouble line. What side of the line are you on?

Money Trouble Line

Spender	Saver/Investor
In Debt	No Debt
No Spending Plan	Has Spending Plan
No Emergency Fund	Full Emergency Fund
Depreciating Liabilities	Appreciating Assets
(90% are here)	(10% are here)

The goal of this book is to help you move closer to the right side of the trouble line. Very few people are there. Some may have lots of income. They are income statement rich but they spend more than they make so they are actually broke. Then there are others who make much less money, but spend even less, and they are balance sheet rich. They know how to handle money.

You can achieve your financial dreams. You need the education and perspective to help you get there. It's not easy, and it's not fast. Get over it. No matter what your situation is – start now!

It's your money. Keep more of it.

The Problem

People are working harder while incomes go down and expenses go up. Why?

- **Tough Job Market.** The U.S. has lost nearly 3 million private-sector jobs over the past three years. More than 8 million Americans are looking for work. In 2003, the U.S. trade deficit broke $500 billion as we lost jobs overseas.

- **Less Income.** The median household income fell by over $1,400 over the past two years. Workers had fewer hours on the job.

- **Health Care Costs.** Health insurance premiums have increased 50% over the last three years, and 14% last year alone. Workers are facing higher co-pays, deductibles, and other cost sharing, with no relief in sight.

- **College Tuition Hikes.** Average college tuition has grown far faster than family incomes. Many universities raised tuition by 20 percent or more this year.

- **Predatory Lending.** Irresponsible financial institutions rob people blind with outrageous fees and misleading "deals".

- **Lack of Education.** We never received the education we need to manage money well. Most of us are in the dark when it comes to money.

9

The Impact

- 70% of us live paycheck to paycheck, regardless of income.
- 92% of disposable income goes to pay debt.
- 62% of us retire on less than $10,000 per year.
- 51% of all Americans have no retirement savings.
- We now average over $28,400 in non-mortgage debt.
- 62% of Americans say money is their biggest problem.
- The number one stress employees face at work is money.
- Money is a major cause of divorce.
- 75% of us will have a significant negative economic event every 10 years.
- Of those eligible for an Individual Retirement Account only 7% have one.

The Solution - Education

To build a solid financial future you need to understand the basic metrics of money management. If you don't know these and apply these in your every day living, you will never get ahead of the game.

The 5 fundamental things you need to understand are:

1. **Money Math** – What makes money active?

2. **Credit Cards** – The biggest source of financial drag.

3. **Spending Plan** – Know where your money goes.

4. **Dump Debt** – How to really dump all debt.

5. **Home Loans** – Save money and take control.

Once you have the basics down, you can move on to more sophisticated financial matters like which Mutual Fund to invest in or how to lower your tax bill. Without the basic fundamentals covered you will always struggle with money. It is like Maslow's hierarchy of needs.

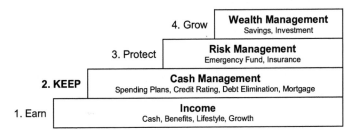

This book is focused on step 2, how to keep more of the money you earn. Until you master this step, nothing much can happen long-term.

The Financial Cycle

In the 1960s, MIT economist Franco Modigliani created a household financial life cycle model. In 1985, he won the Nobel Prize in Economics for this work.

The graph shows income versus expenses for a typical household from age 20 through retirement.

The income deficit comes from mortgages, credit card debt, auto loans, children, toys, health care, education, and more. From my own experience, the surplus in the early years is probably quite a bit smaller than it was in the 1960's.

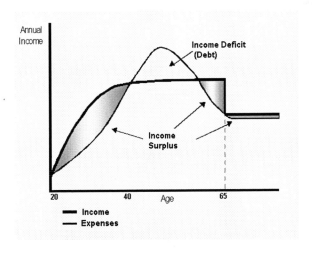

What would happen if you had a sharp drop in income at age 36 because of a layoff? How about an unexpected child at 38; or an injury or major medical issue at age 45? What would happen to expenses? How do your income and expenses compare to this graph? What happens if expenses and debt load don't come down by retirement age? How can you get control? Read on.

1) MONEY MATH

There are two basic forces that make money move in value; Compound Interest and Inflation.

Compound Interest

Compound Interest can be either your best friend or your worst enemy. It is your friend when you invest money and it gains value through compound interest. It is your enemy when you have credit card debt, a car loan, or any other debt.

Here is an example of the power of compound interest. If I start with One Penny and double it every day for 30 days, how much do I end up with? At the end of 30 days I will have **$5,368,709.12.** Wish I could do that trick every month.

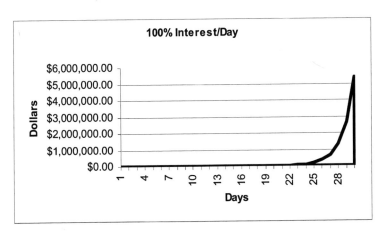

This is the graph of <u>One Penny</u> doubled every day for a month. Why do people feel that saving is pointless? Look at the first 25 days. Flat as a pancake. No action noticeable. After day 25 it takes off. Most people don't have the patience with their money to see it through. Most of the real increase is at the end. We want it up front.

If you could save $250 per month for 20 years at 10% compound interest you would have $189,842, and only $60,000 would have been your cash contribution. Triple your money, not bad.

It's Interest on Interest

Simple Interest

There are two basic kinds of interest: simple and compound. Simple interest is figured once. If you loaned $300 to a friend for one month and charged her 1% interest ($3), you'd be dealing with simple interest.

Compound Interest

Compound interest is a little different. With compound interest, the money you earn in interest becomes part of the principal, and also starts to earn interest. If you loaned that same friend $300 for one year and charged her 1% each month until the end of the year (12% annually), you'd be using compound interest. At the end of the first month, she would owe you $303. At the end of the second month, she would owe you $306.03. At the end of the third month, she would owe you $309.09, and so on.

Compound interest is part of what makes credit cards and loans so difficult to pay off. The rules of interest are the same ones that increase your savings over time, but with credit card debt they're in the creditor's favor—not in yours. With some rates as high as 25%, collecting interest on credit card loans could be viewed as legal loan sharking. As you can tell, it's a lucrative business.

Inflation

You had a compelling and fascinating discussion about inflation over a beer when out with your friends just last Friday, right? Not a chance. Nobody talks about inflation any more. Yet it is an important concept and number to keep track of. Inflation will tell you how much extra money you are losing if you have debt or how much real money you are making in your investments.

14

Inflation is what you get when the overall price of goods and services increases and the purchasing power of money drops. Deflation is the opposite, when prices decrease. The important point here is:

As inflation rises, every dollar you have buys a smaller amount of goods or services.

The buying power of money is more important than how much money you have. It's a relative thing. Hey, isn't that an Einstein thing? If you have debt you have debt payments, which means you have less money. So with debt and inflation you lose money extra fast.

Over the last 30 years inflation has averaged about 3%. As long as income and investments outpace inflation, you are getting ahead of the game.

The "Real" Interest Rate

What we really want to know is the "real" interest rate. It is a combination of Inflation and Compound Interest. It can be expressed this way:

Real Interest Rate = Average Interest Rate – Inflation Rate

If you have investments that return 5% and the inflation rate is 2%, then you are really getting 3% rate of return on your money.

Money is Active

The key concept here is that money is ACTIVE. Compound Interest and Inflation are always at work to make money move in a positive or negative direction. The value of money and the amount of money you have is always changing. If you do not act on your money, it will act on you, and not always in a positive way. If you do not control your money, it will control you.

Assets / Liabilities/Net Worth

An asset puts money in your pocket. A liability takes it out. If you borrow money to buy something you pay interest on that item. If this asset does not appreciate faster than the debt interest rate, you are losing money. If you pay interest on something that depreciates, you are losing twice. If you add inflation you have three strikes. You're outa here! No wonder money seems to slip through our fingers.

The goal is to:

1. **Maximize Appreciating Assets**. They increase your net worth. (Like Real Estate, Securities such as stocks and bonds, and some Life Insurance products)

2. **Minimize Depreciating Liabilities**. They decrease your net worth and take money away from you. (Like credit cards, car loans, furniture loans, payday loans)

Imagine what it would be like to have nothing but appreciating assets. Everything else has been paid for in cash. No credit card debt. It can be done.

The first step is to know where you are. A statement of financial position is a great tool to do that. First you add up your assets, then add up your liabilities, after that subtract liabilities from assets and you end up with net worth. It will give you a clear picture of appreciating assets versus depreciating liabilities. It looks like this:

ASSETS
Cash/Cash Equivalents

Checking Account Balance	
Savings Account Balance	
Money Market Acct. Balance	
Certificate of Deposit Balance	
Treasury Bill Value	
Savings Bonds Value	
Other Value	
Sub-Total	

Invested Assets

Stocks	
Bonds	
Mutual Funds	
IRA	
Vested Portion of Retirement	
401k	
Other Invested Assets	
Sub-Total	

Daily Use Assets
(Things used every day)

Home Value	
Vehicles	
Personal Property	
Other Use Assets	
Sub-Total	

TOTAL ASSETS	

LIABILITIES

Mortgage Balance	
Credit Card Debt	
Vehicle Loan Balances	
Other Debt Balances	
TOTAL LIABILITIES	

Assets - Liabilities = $_____ Net Worth

You want this to be a positive number. If it isn't, you may need a debt elimination plan and a few other things to get you back on track.

2) CREDIT CARDS

> "Life was a lot simpler when what we honored was father and mother rather than all major credit cards."
>
> Robert Orben

Financial Drag

Until the mid 1970's there were usury laws that limited the interest rate banks and others could charge. This kept the loan sharks away. Once the laws changed, Pandora's box was open. Once the banks did the math with higher interest rates they knew they could make huge amounts of money off of people who were impatient or ignorant.

Credit cards are designed to keep you poor. They work the math to keep you hooked. Between the minimum payment and declining amortization, they have you in their grasp. Credit card debt creates the most drag on finances. You can't get velocity on your money with credit card debt hanging around. All credit card debt has to go. Here's why.

Minimum Payments

The first concept you should know about is the minimum payment. It's the minimum amount you are required to pay each month. This is usually equal to around 2% of your average balance due. So, if your average daily balance for a certain month is $500, your minimum payment for that month will be $10. This probably sounds like a good deal until you remember that you're also paying interest on that $500. If you're being charged an interest rate of 18% on the balance of $500, that $10 won't go far towards paying off the balance. This is how most credit card companies make their money. By requiring that you pay only very small amounts each month, they know that it will take you much longer to pay off your debt, and that you'll end up paying a lot more interest over time.

Here is an example based on a $5,000 balance and 17% interest rate.

Card	Minimum Payment %	Monthly Payment	Interest Cost	Years Until Paid
A	1.67%	$83.50	$25,354	81
B	2.00%	$100.00	$11,304	40
C	2.50%	$125.00	$6,210	24
D	3.00%	$150.00	$4,296	18

The lower the minimum payment, the longer it takes, and the more it costs.

Credit Cards and Declining Payments

Did you know that a 2.99% credit card is effectively a 17% loan? There is a big difference between credit cards and regular loans.

Credit cards are based on a declining payment schedule. You pay 1.5% to 3% of the outstanding balance every month. As the balance comes down, so does the payment. While this sounds like a great deal on the surface, look what happens.

Declining Payments - Credit Card

Payment #	Balance	Payment	Interest	Principal	New Balance
12	$1,874	$47	$28	$19	$1,855
24	$1,655	$42	$24	$18	$1,637
36	$1,461	$37	$21	$16	$1,445
48	$1,289	$33	$19	$14	$1,275
60	$1,138	$29	$17	$12	**$1,126**

At the end of five years of payments, you still have $1,126 left on the balance. You paid around $2,256 to lower your balance only $748.

A home or auto loan is based on a level payment schedule. You pay the same amount for a fixed time frame. Look at the difference.

19

Level Payments - Home Loan

Payment #	Balance	Payment	Interest	Principal	New Balance
12	$1,843	$53	$27	$26	$1,817
24	$1,510	$53	$22	$31	$1,479
36	$1,113	$53	$16	$37	$1,076
48	$638	$53	$9	$44	$594
60	$72	$53	$1	$52	**$20**

At the ends of five years you only have $20 dollars left to pay. What happened? Lets look at them together.

Declining – Credit Card

Payment #	Balance	Payment	Interest	Principal	New Balance
12	$1,874	$47	$28	$19	$1,855
24	$1,655	$42	$24	$18	$1,637
36	$1,461	$37	$21	$16	$1,445
48	$1,289	$33	$19	$14	$1,275
60	$1,138	$29	$17	$12	**$1,126**

Level Payments – Home Loan

Payment #	Balance	Payment	Interest	Principal	New Balance
12	$1,843	$53	$27	$26	$1,817
24	$1,510	$53	$22	$31	$1,479
36	$1,113	$53	$16	$37	$1,076
48	$638	$53	$9	$44	$594
60	$72	$53	$1	$52	**$20**

Notice with the credit card declining payment, the payment changes (decreases) but the ratio of principal to interest paid stays the same at about 60% interest and 40% principal.

With the level payment, the payment stays the same but the ratio of principal to interest changes. It starts out with a low percentage going to pay principal, and ends up with a very high percentage going towards principal.

Here is another example. The credit card loan is here:

Credit Card Loan	
Balance	$30,000
Average Monthly Payment	$101
Payback Time (Yrs)	30
Stated Interest Rate	2.99%
Effective Rate	
Interest Paid	$6,214
Total Payments	$36,214
Effective Interest Rate	17.16%

2.99% sounds pretty good if you don't look too far down the road. The 2.99% credit card is really a 17% loan. Why? Declining payments and low minimum payments. The chapter on how to Dump Debt shows you should get out of this trap.

Here is another example:

Credit Card Loan	
Balance	$30,000
Average Monthly Payment	$107
Payback Time (Yrs)	55
Stated Interest Rate	9.99%
Effective Rate	
Interest Paid	$40,867
Total Payments	$70,867
Effective Interest Rate	57.67%

So here a 9.99% credit card is effectively a 57% loan. How can you hang on to your money if you are paying these kinds of rates? You can't. And just so we know what we missed, $101 per month invested at 10% for 30 years yields $228,309; and $107 per month for 55 years yields $3,058,211.

So let's tackle another aspect of credit cards. Why does the credit card balance never seem to go down? Same answer. Here it is. I start with a $2,100 credit card balance and I don't charge anything for 3 months. Then I see a sale and charge a little something. Not much, just $60 worth, I needed it, whatever it was. Nothing again for another 90 days but then my car has a minor malfunction and I charge the repair.

Payment #	Balance	Payment	Interest	Principal	New Balance
1	$2,100	$53	$32	$21	$2,079
2	$2,078	$52	$31	$21	$2,057
3	$2,057	$51	$31	$20	$2,037
	New Purchase				$60
	New Balance				$2,097

Payment #	Balance	Payment	Interest	Principal	New Balance
4	$2,097	$51	$32	$19	$2,078
5	$2,078	$50	$31	$19	$2,059
6	$2,057	$50	$31	$19	$2,038
	New Purchase				$60
	New Balance				$2,098

So in 6 months I'm $307 out of pocket. I purchased $120 worth of stuff. I paid $187 in interest. And the balance is back where I started. Great stuff for the credit card companies, really bad for my financial picture. This is the biggest reason that people feel like they don't know where their money goes.

Balance & Finance Charges

Another method to drain more money from you is to use different ways to calculate the finance charges for your monthly balance. There are 3 ways most credit card companies use to do this. They are Average Daily Balance that excludes new purchases, Average Daily Balance that includes new purchases, and Two-Cycle Average Daily Balance that includes new purchases. Here is an example of what you might pay for each:

	Finance Charges
Average Daily Balance (excluding new purchases)	$40.00
Average Daily Balance (including new purchases)*	$80.00
Two-cycle Average Daily Balance (including new purchases)	$120.00

Look on the back of your credit card statement and see if you have a Two-Cycle card. If you do, you might consider dumping that one.

Mental Accounting

The "debtly" behavior associated with credit cards is Mental Accounting. This is the tendency to value some dollars less than others and in doing so waste them. We categorize money and use money differently depending on where it comes from, what form it takes, and how it is spent. If you have $75.00 in your wallet and you pay $50.00 for something, you see and feel that money going away. If you whip out the plastic, there is no sense of spending real money, of real loss. You just handed over a plastic card and got it back again along with the purchased item.

We also tend to relax our discipline when we are making lots of small purchases. Five bucks here, ten bucks there, and pretty soon we are talking about real money.

"Credit cards make us poorer because we are more likely to spend, and more likely to spend poorly. Credit cards will cause you to spend money you would not ordinarily spend."

Why Smart People Make Big Money Mistakes, Belsky & Gilovich, 1999

How To Counter Mental Accounting?

- Pay cash more often.
- Think in terms of "Every dollar spends the same".
- Be patient, think over you purchases, especially big ones.

- Track what you spend, watch the number of small purchases.

One client I talked with had made a number of sophisticated investments; a wine collection worth a few hundred thousand dollars, three of four hundred thousand in stocks, and over $300,000 in credit card debt. He thought it was "cheap" money because the interest rates were all below 4%. He did not know what you know now. He was a former bank executive.

One more thing. Everyone says that they pay off their credit card balance at the end of the month, but the credit card companies tell us that most of us do not, and they are glad for it. It keeps them rich. It's another version of mental accounting.

Tricks

Some credit card companies use all kinds of tricks and gimmicks to get you in and keep you addicted to credit. Here are some gimmicks to watch out for:

- **Bait and Switch** – Zero percent interest for the Pope, everyone else pays more.

- **Late Fees** - They change the billing address and watch the late fees pile up.

- **Mileage Plans** – Be $50,000 in debt and get a free trip across the country as long as you leave on alternate Thursdays when the moon shines.

- **Cash Advance Rates** –Rates around 25% for this one.

- **Low Minimum Payments** – Keeps you paying longer and more money down the drain.

- **Balance Transfer Fees** – Switch over to the 0% rate and get hammered on fees.

- **Zero Percent Interest** – For 6 months or until you make one late payment.

- **Universal Default Clause** – Pay some other bill late and watch your credit card interest rate skyrocket.

- **No Grace Period** - A 20-day grace period on purchases instead of 30 days.

You can also download 20 Sneaky Credit Card Tricks from www.Money-Metrics.com

How to Fight Back

Fight back and dump debt by doing some of the following:

- **Pay twice/month.** Split your payment because it can reduce the amount of interest you pay.
- **Pay more than the minimum.** The more you pay, the less it costs long term.
- **Keep your payments at the same level;** don't reduce them as the minimum payment comes down.
- **Don't Use Credit Cards.** Cut them up and pay cash or use a debit card.
- **Get a Debt Elimination Plan** – Get rid of debt fast.

For your Debt Elimination Plan and more on Credit Cards visit www.Money-Metrics.com.

3) SPENDING PLAN

"If you know how to spend less than you get, you have the philosopher's stone."

Benjamin Franklin

To manage money you need to know how to save, spend, and invest successfully. A spending plan is essential if you are going to manage money well. This is just a list of your income and a list of where you spend your money - your outgo. When you have this plan it becomes much easier to see where you can save money, spend less, get out of debt, and invest for the future.

Income

Step 1. Know Your Income. Write down every source of income.
Income can be looked at as being either Active or Passive. Active Income is where I work for my money, and Passive Income is where my money works for me. In the early years most people are in the active income mode. When you are older and have saved and invested you are in the passive income mode. If you have credit card debt you have to work extra long and hard to pay it off and get to the passive mode.

Step 2. Know <u>Where</u> You Spend Money. Write it down. Get a little notebook and write down everything you spend for a month, every penny. You may be surprised at where your money really goes. At the end of each line item spent, place a + sign to indicate whether you feel this purchase brought you good value for money spent or a – sign to indicate that it was not good value for money spent. This helps you get conscious about your spending. Spend on purpose, not unconsciously.

Step 3. Set Personal Goals & Objectives. What do you really want to do and have? When do you want it? How much money will it take? Short-term goals will happen in a year. Long-term goals are out 2 or more years. These will keep you moving forward when it becomes a real grind.

Step 4. Develop a Spending Plan. Start with the Basic Spending Plan and then move on to the Detailed Plan. Given your income, do you have enough to cover basic expenses? Sample basic and detailed plans are available at www.money-Metrics.com on the "downloads" page.

Outgo

Lets talk about where we spend money for a minute. Outgoing money can be put into three buckets.

1. Right Now - Cash Management

These are the day-to-day expenses. What you have to deal with right now. This includes necessities like Housing, Utilities, Transportation, Food, Clothing, Insurance, and credit card debt payments.

2. Don't Want - Risk Management

Here you want to avoid the big problems, and I mean big like serious health issues, fire, and other accidents. Transfer the risk of what you don't want to have happen. Risk management is about transferring the risk of a catastrophic event. Remember that 75% of us will have a significant negative financial event every 10 years. See your insurance professional for more information. At least try to have health, homeowners, and auto insurance. Other insurance needs may include Life, Disability, and Long-Term Care.

One of the biggest reasons people get into trouble is that they have a major event and no insurance or no emergency fund. Do your best to get this covered. Even with just $2,000 in an emergency fund you can increase your deductibles, which will make the insurance cheaper and free up money for other uses, like paying off debt.

3. Do Want - Future Management

Once you have 1 and 2 covered, put money away for what you do want to have happen. This is the realm of Financial Planners and Advisors. When you are out of debt, except the mortgage, you should talk to one of these professionals about where to invest.

The goal is to get to where you can invest at least 15% of your income. I personally like good mutual funds that can return 10% or better over time.

Your goals and objectives (Retirement, College, Dreams/Goals, Passive Income) will help define the investments that are right for you. Future Management also includes these topics:

- Retirement Plan
- Will / Estate Plan
- Tax Reduction Plan
- Teach Your Children – pass along what you have learned about money.

Had a client who was wealthy - but apparently not too organized. He was a multi-millionaire with bad credit. He just didn't pay much attention to his spending. He was late with the mortgage and the Porsche and the credit card payments. When it came time to get a new loan, he paid a much higher rate and went through a lot of hassles to get his credit straightened out. It cost him a lot of money.

Basic Spending Plan

At a minimum, know what your basic living
necessities include:

Item	A
HOUSING	
First Mortgage	
2nd/HELOC	
Repairs/Fees	
UTILITIES	
Electricity	
Water	
Gas	
Phone	
Trash	
TRANSPORTATION	
Car Payment 1	
Car Payment 2	
Gas & Oil	
Repairs & Tires	
FOOD	
Groceries	
Dining Out	
CLOTHING	
Adults	
Children	
INSURANCE	
Homeowners	
Health/Medical	
Life & Other	
Car Insurance	
CREDIT CARD DEBT	
Total Basic Outgo	
Gross Monthly Income	
Balance	

up and subtract the total form gross income. What is left? es out and what's left? Is that how much money you really eft at the end of the month? If not, where does it go? Most ple are missing hundred's if not thousands of dollars. Find that oney. Hunt's on!

Percentages

Average percentages of expense compared to overall income might look like this:

Item	Percent
Savings	15%
Medical/Health	10%
Other Insurance	5%
Housing	35%
Utilities	5%
Food	10%
Transportation	10%
Clothing	5%
Lifestyle	5%
(Debt	**0%)**

Do the basic spending plan first, and then tackle the detailed spending plan. See if you are in the ballpark with these average percentages. If not, maybe there is something you can do about it.

A spending plan helps you think through what is important to you. How much of what you spend money on is for survival, or for comforts, or for luxuries? How much is spent for stuff you really don't really want, don't really use, and really can't afford? Know where you personal "enough" line is.

A detailed spending plan can be found at www.Money-Metrics.com on the Downloads page.

Avoid Big Number Bias

Another "debtly" behavior that gets us into trouble is a bias towards big numbers. We miss the small numbers and percentages that really add up. Check bills and statements for unexplained or unwanted charges. Get picky about it; it's your money.

Here is an example of saving ideas

Don't buy a new car	$ 250
Eat out less	$ 25
Buy less clothes	$ 75
Fewer trips/vacations	$ 50
Lattes	$ 50
Cell Phone	$ 100
Sub-total monthly savings:	**$ 975**
Pay off credit cards	**$ 350**
(based on average $18,700 credit card debt)	
Total Monthly Savings	**$ 1,325**

The savings over time is:

Average annual savings	**$ 15,900**
Savings after 5 years	**$ 79,500**
Value after 10 years	**$242,403**
Value after 20 years	**$780,452**
(Note: Calculated at 8% ROI)	

Save a little money here and there and it can really add up.

4) DUMP DEBT

> "The rich rule over the poor and the borrower is servant to the lender."
>
> Proverbs 22:7

Debt is the biggest threat to your financial success. It is financial cancer. If you have Credit Card debt on a depreciating liability (like clothes, cars, boats, sporting goods, etc, etc, etc.) you are throwing your money away. Debt is a big wet blanket over your future. It looks so easy and good now, but can kill your future plans and ruin your life. Get rid of all debt. OK, except the mortgage.

5 Steps to Dump Debt

1. Develop a Spending Plan.

You have tracked you spending for 30 days, done your Basic Plan, and hopefully the Detailed Plan. You now have a much better idea of where you money goes. You have probably found some money that you can put towards credit card debt.

2. Stop borrowing money/don't use credit cards.

Put away the credit cards. Cut them up or whatever you have to do to not use them again. If you don't pay cash, don't buy it.

3. Put $1,000 - $2,000 in an Emergency Fund.

Save up about $2,000 as your temporary emergency fund. This will keep you from reaching for the plastic when something relatively minor happens. If you need to use this money, hold off paying any exta on anything else until this fund is back to $2,000.

4. Pay off all debt (except the mortgage).

Get on a debt elimination plan. Use the level payment and debt snowball method (or other method) to pay down debt as quickly as possible. Know how much to pay on each debt until they are gone.

5. Save enough for a full Emergency Fund (6 months of basic expenses)

After you have this accomplished you will have money available for investing, retirement and other purposes.

Emergency Funds

One of the biggest reasons people get into financial trouble is they failed to have an emergency fund. When life happens to them, the financial house of cards falls down. When you have an emergency fund the bumps in the road of life don't turn into sink holes, or cause a major wreck, they stay speed bumps. Emergency funds are part of your overall risk management plan.

Pay Off Debt

The spending plan gives you the chance to find money to pay down your debt faster. Managed money always goes farther. With a little extra money there are a number of ways to attack debt.

- **Pay Off Lowest Balance First**
- **Pay Off Highest Interest Rate First**
- **Pay Off Biggest Finance Charge First**
- **Debt Snowball**

When you run the numbers, they all come out very close. It matters more which way you will stick with rather than which one saves you more money on paper.

Debt Snowball Example

Here is an example of a Debt Snowball.

Item	Balance	Payment	Snowball Payment
Sears	$300	$15	
VISA	$2,000	$60	$75
M.C.	$7,500	$200	$275
Car Loan	$9,000	$250	$525
Total Paid/Month		**$525**	

The idea is to pay a small debt off first, put that payment towards the next debt, put both of those towards the next one, and so on until they are all paid off. This increases the amount paid towards each balance and can get rid of debt quickly.

The normal payoff time for this scenario would be 15 years and 5 months at an effective interest rate of over 24%. With the debt snowball the payoff time is 3 years and 5 months at an effective rate of just over 10%.

There are other ways to attack debt. Go to www.Money-Metrics.com for a free Debt Elimination Plan.

Get the Snowball Rolling

Here are some ideas to get the snowball rolling:

- The spending plan gives you the chance to find extra money. Managed money always goes farther.
- Sell something.
- With an emergency fund you could increase insurance deductibles and put that saved money towards the snowball.
- Get radical, think outside the box, get mad at debt. Something will come to you to help if you put emotion behind it.
- Don't give up, stay with the program, and remember your goals and objectives.

5) HOME LOANS

> "Where we love is home, home that our feet may leave, but not our hearts."
>
> Oliver Wendell Holmes

About 50% of Americans own a home and most of them don't want to think much about the mortgage payment. That is usually a very costly mistake. Money is active, and that means the money in your home is moving. If you want to just get a 30-year fixed loan and forget about it, you will probably throw thousands if not tens of thousands of dollars down the drain. The home loan is the largest single payment you make. It's your biggest asset (the home itself) and liability (the loan payment). Pay attention to it.

If you are part of the 50% who do not own a home, get pre-approved for a home loan to see where you are. The process will tell you if you are ready, and you may be pleasantly surprised, or what you need to do to be ready. Either way it is free and good information to know.

Mortgage Basics

Many people describe the mortgage loan process as a tangled maze, difficult to navigate. The following is an introduction to mortgages, how lenders decide whether or not to lend money and some things to watch out for to make sure you get the best loan possible.

What is a Mortgage?

A mortgage is actually the stack of paperwork and legal documents that you sign to get a loan to buy or refinance your property. Mortgages make your property the security against the loan. If you don't keep your promise to pay the loan on time, it gives the lender the right to take the steps necessary to sell your property to satisfy the debt, to foreclose on you. Most mortgages on the west coast are actually Deeds of Trust. A Deed of Trust makes it easier for the lender to foreclose on your property, in case of default.

Mortgage Insurance

Mortgage insurance protects the lender from any losses they might incur from default and foreclosure. You pay for it, but it only benefits the lender. Avoid this if you can. Do a first mortgage for up to 80%, then a second mortgage or equity line of credit for the balance.

Pre-Payment Penalty

A Pre-Payment Penalty is the lenders way of making sure that they make their money off you before you refinance or move. Read the fine print. Make sure you know if your loan has a pre-payment penalty. Only take a loan with a pre-payment penalty if you know you are going to be in the home at least as long as the penalty time. Loans with pre-payment penalties will usually have a slightly lower interest rate, so they can be useful in the right circumstances.

What Things Affect Your Loan?

There are a number of factors that affect your loan. The biggest concerns are:

- Interest Rate
- Down Payment
- Closing Costs/Loan Fees/Rebate Points
- Credit Score
- Debt to Income Ratios
- Loan to Value Ratios
- Appraisal

Credit & Loan Approval

Lenders look at these three major areas for loan approval:

- Credit (credit score, payment history)
- Capacity (income and employment history)
- Collateral (assets, house value)

Lenders also view it this way:

- Income – do you have the earnings history to repay the loan?
- Debt – how much non-mortgage debt you owe?
- Credit – what is your credit score and credit history?
- Savings – how much in the bank, IRA, or elsewhere?
- Ratios – Debt to Income ratios and Loan to Value ratios.
- Collateral – is the property value high enough?

Credit Scores

Your credit score is based on a mathematical formula developed by Fair, Isaac & Company in California. It is commonly referred to as your FICO score. Most lenders are using this score as a major factor in deciding whether to lend money or not.

Credit scores are based roughly on:

- Age of credit (about 15%)
- Mix of credit (about 10%)
- Amount of balance (about 30%)
- Payment history (about 35%)
- Recent credit inquiries (about 10%)

Credit scores range from 350 to 850. If you have a credit score over 720 you are in great shape. 680 to 720 is very good. 620 to 680 is OK. Lower than 620 is marginal. Loans can be found for almost any credit score down to 500 and even for bankruptcies that have just been discharged.

Mortgage Risk Scale

Lenders balance interest rates against risk. The higher the risk, the higher the rate. It's very much like a teeter-totter or a scale. Push down on one end, the other end goes up.

Lenders equate higher risk, and charge higher interest rates, for the following:

- No money down or less than 20% down
- Late mortgage payments
- Late credit card payments
- Poor credit scores
- No verification of income or assets.
- Frequent employment changes
- Frequent address changes
- Bankruptcy in the recent past
- High debt to income ratios (too much debt for the income)

Mortgage Do's

Pay attention to your mortgage. When it comes to a home purchase or refinance:

- **Know your purpose** – Lower Payment, Debt Elimination, Investment.
- **Know your time frame** – How long will you be in this house?
- **Know your loan options** - Watch out for the "debtly" behavior – anchors.
- **Know the ROI** – Do the math.
- **Know your credit score** – Make sure it is accurate.
- **Know how much you can borrow** - Get pre-approved.

The biggest point here is to have some idea of how long you will stay in a home. Remember that most people move every 7 years.

Mortgage Don'ts

Avoid These:

- **Mortgage Insurance.** Explore other solutions.
- **Bait and Switch.** No fees, no closing costs, and an unbelievable rate are reserved for the Pope.
- **Shopping for Rates** – Any quote over the phone about rates and closing costs is worthless. The only way to know for sure what you can get is to complete an application, have your credit report reviewed, and get a Good Faith Estimate.
- **Excessive Fees (Front/Back)** – Ask about the Yield Spread Premium or Rebate Points on your proposed loan.
- **Loan Option Anchors** – Know about other loan options. The 30 year fixed loan is the most expensive loan you can get. If you are not going to live in the house 30 years, explore options.
- **A Loan Officer or Mortgage Broker who is not a Teacher** - If they won't help you clearly understand your options find someone else.

Loan Options

There are lots of different types of loans available today. The old 30-year fixed may not be the loan that is right for you. People stay in a house an average of 5 to 7 years and move. Why would you have a 30-year loan, the most expensive loan you can have, if you don't plan to live there 30 years? Talk with a mortgage broker about loan options and how they can serve you best.

Fixed Rate

30 year, 15 year

The old standby and the most expensive loan you can have. You get the guaranteed rate in trade for a much higher rate.

The "debtly" behavior called Anchors keeps us afraid of other types of loans. If you understand other types (and the Real Interest Rate) they can be excellent financial tools.

Adjustable Rate Mortgage (ARM)

Monthly, 6 month, 1 year, 3/1, 5/1, 7/1

Adjustable Rate Mortgages have been characterized as risky and down-right scary. This is true only for the uneducated and uninformed. Now they come with limits on how far and how fast they can adjust. Some are tied to very slow moving averages or indexes.

When you run the numbers a 1-year ARM has an average interest rate advantage over a 30-year fixed for the first 3 years. A 5/1 ARM (fixed for 5 years) has a 7-year advantage over a 30-year fixed. So what really matters is how long will you stay in that house.

Hybrid ARMs are fixed for a certain period, and then adjust. Lenders sometimes show these as 3/1, fixed for 3 years than adjust annually after that. The interest rates for ARMs are much lower than for fixed rate loans.

Other Loan Types

Stated Income, No Income, No Assets
No points, No Fees, No Cost
Zero-down, 106%, First Time Homebuyer
Poor Credit, Sub-Prime
Option ARM, Cash Flow Loan. The choice of 4 different payments each month: Minimum, Interest Only, 30 year, 15 year.

What can you do with these loan types? Here are some examples:

30 year fixed				
Interest Rate	3.75%	4.75%	6.00%	6.75%
Term	30	30	30	30
Payment (P&I)	$1,389	$1,565	$1,799	$1,946

Old faithful; most expensive, behavioral anchor; sometimes an OK loan for the right person.

Interest Only				
Interest Rate	3.75%	4.75%	6.00%	6.75%
Payment (P&I)	$938	$1,188	$1,500	$1,688

Scary, unknown territory; saves people lots of money; a good loan for many people.

Here is an example:

Monthly Savings				
30 yr versus Interest Only	$452	$377	$299	$258

The maximum monthly savings would be over $1,000 per month between highest 30 year payment and the lowest Interest Only payment.

> If you want to own a home today, you probably can. There are so many loan programs out there to choose from. It does not cost anything to get pre-approved. It will show you what you can afford, or what you need to do to get better prepared. Visit www.Money-Metrics.com for a free pre-approval.

Here is an example of how these monthly savings can be used. This client had credit card debt that was getting to be a burden. They wanted out from under the stress.

Item	Total	Rate	Monthly
Mortgage	$300,000	4.75%	$1,565
Debt	$25,000	Average 9.99%	$500
			$2,065

Item	Total	Rate	Monthly
Mortgage	$300,000	6% IO	$1,625
Debt	$0	$0	$0
			$1,625

	Monthly Savings	$440

You can see they took a higher interest rate loan that was an Interest Only payment (had to, their credit score had gone down), eliminated all debt, and still came out ahead by $440 per month.

Your home loan should not be about interest rate. It should be viewed as part of your overall financial strategy. Use it to your best advantage, not the lenders. You should control your mortgage, instead of your mortgage controlling you.

Important Ratios

DTI – Debt to Income. Total debt payments divided by gross income. Usually 50% is the maximum to get a loan. Lenders like to see this as low as possible.

LTV – Loan to Value. Loan Amount divided by Appraised Value. Over 80% costs more. Less the 80% and lenders feel safer only because they can sell your house easier and faster for 80% of total value.

"No Cost" loans

"No cost" loans do not exist. The interest rate is just increased to cover the costs. Remember rebate points? This is one way they can be used. You pay for it for the life of the loan through a higher interest rate. It can be the right loan for you if you are not staying in the house very long. Know your purpose and your time frame.

Credit Repair

How do you repair your credit rating?

1. **Correct any mistakes on your report.**
2. **Pay your existing bills on time.**
3. **Reduce your debt.**
4. **Wait**

Unfortunately there are no quick and easy fixes for low credit scores. The most important thing to do is pay your existing bills on time. If you can manage it, after doing your spending plan, try to pay down the balances on any debt. Keep at it and check you credit report every 6 months or so. Also, make sure to get any incorrect information on your credit report removed or corrected.

To get your credit report and credit score please contact:

- TransUnion 800-888-4213 or www.transunion.com

- Equifax 800-685-1111 or www.equifax.com

- Experian 888-397-3742 or www.experian.com

Loan Fees

Front-End Fees

Mortgage brokers and banks charge a fee for their services. This fee varies from 1 to 2 percent of the loan. Banks charge the same fees as a broker but sometimes roll them into the loan and hide them from you. Bank or broker, they need to be paid for the service of processing your loan. These are referred to as front-end or origination fees.

Back-End Fees

Lenders can also compensate a broker or loan officer when they deliver a loan in a way that is invisible to the borrower. These are called "rebate points" or back-end fees. They are reflected in the interest rate to the borrower. The higher the rebate points, the higher the interest rate. This is where loan officers play the game of "I can get you that loan for less". They are really just doing a shell game on you.

Junk Fees

Junk fees are another way lenders make more money off of you. Some examples of junk fees are "affiliate consulting fee", "amortization fee", "bank inspection fee", "lender's inspection fee", "settlement fee", "signup fee", "funding fee", "lender's attorney fee", "endorsement fee", "express mail fee", "document preparation fee", "notary fee", "messenger fee", "photograph fee", "assumption fee", "administrative fee", "document review fee", and "translation fee". Look out for these on you documents and question the loan officer until he gives up and removes them.

Par & Points

A "point" is mortgage mumbo for 1% of the loan amount. PAR means there are no points being paid to anyone for the given loan. The table below is an example of a loan with a PAR rate of 5.125%. The rebate points are in parenthesis and reflect the money paid to the loan officer.

To get the 5.000% rate you would have to pay .375% of the loan amount up front.

If a loan officer can talk you into this loan program at the 6.000% interest rate they pocket $4,125. If they did not tell you about this what do you call it? I call it stealing your money. You pay for this for the life of the loan through a higher interest rate.

Rates	Points/Rebate	Loan Amt $300,000
4.875	0.875	$2,625
5.000	0.375	$1,125
5.125	**0.000**	**$0 (par)**
5.250	(0.375)	($1,125)
5.375	(0.625)	($1,875)
5.500	(0.875)	($2,625)
5.625	(1.000)	($3,000)
5.750	(1.125)	($3,375)
5.875	(1.250)	($3,750)
6.000	(1.375)	($4,125)
6.125	(1.500)	($4,500)

When you are dealing with loan officers ask them what the PAR rate is or ask them how much rebate they are getting. Compare all loans and fees at the PAR rate.

Leverage

Any homeowner or would-be homeowner should know a little about leverage. It is part of what makes owning a home, or many homes, financially attractive.

If I invest $10,000 and get a 10% return, I gain $1,000 per year. Good.

Now, if I invest that $10,000 as part of the down payment on a house worth $200,000 and the house appreciates at 4%, my annual gain is measured on the value of the house, $200,000, not just the $10,000. So I will gain $8,000 per year in value on $10,000 invested. That is an effective 80% return. Much better. Not magic, just basic math.

It looks like this:

Invest	Total Value	ROI	1 Yr Gain	1 Year ROI
$10,000	$10,000	10%	$1,000	10%
$10,000	$200,000	4%	$8,000	80%

Year 2 even looks better

Invest	Total Value	ROI	2 Yr Gain	2 Year ROI
$10,000	$10,000	10%	$2,000	20%
$10,000	$200,000	4%	$16,320	163%

More Leverage

Let's say I have $15,068 in credit card debt and my payments are $273 per month. This will take me 33 years to pay off at the minimum payment. I also have a house payment of $1,498 per month (on a 6.0% 30 year fixed loan on $250,000). Total payments are $1,771 per month.

I decide to get out of debt and refinance the home loan. My new loan balance is $265,068 and I have an Interest Only payment now of $994 per month.

Fast-forward ten years. I have invested the difference of $777 and in ten years come out with $159,164. I have paid $119,280 in interest from my interest only loan.

If I had not done anything, by now I would have paid $151,481 in interest, still be making credit card payments and have $0.00 in investment return. The total difference is $191,365. It's your money. Keep more of it.

Looks like this if you do nothing:

Item	Amt	Per Month	10 Years
Debt	$15,068	$273	
Mortgage (30 yr)	$250,000	$1,498	
Interest		$1,771	**$151,481**

Change the picture and...

Item	Amt	Per Month	10 Years
Mortgage (Int. only)	$265,068	$994	**$119,280**
Interest Savings		$777	**$32,201**
Investment Return			**$159,164**
		Total Gain	**$191,365**

Gotta love those six-figure gainers.

46

Closing Costs

Here are some average closing costs. (* Watch out for the junk fees.)

LENDER/BROKER FEES			
	Highest	Lowest	Average
Points (in dollars)	$3,148	$225	$1,038
Administration fee *	$600	$325	$336
Application fee *	$350	$200	$205
Commitment fee *	$660	$295	$498
Document preparation *	$400	$25	$194
Funding fee *	$375	$200	$228
Mortgage broker/lender fee	$1,161	$150	$839
Processing	$595	$37	$320
Tax Service	$100	$60	$73
Underwriting	$749	$100	$269
Wire transfer	$45	$15	$31
THIRD-PARTY FEES			
	Highest	Lowest	Average
Appraisal	$600	$250	$327
Attorney or settlement fees *	$1,423	$50	$445
Credit report	$55	$8.50	$29
Flood certification	$25	$10	$17
Pest & other inspection	$200	$30	$68
Postage/courier	$100	$25	$45
Survey *	$400	$50	$174
Title insurance	$2,075	$50	$605
Title work *	$625	$25	$200
GOVERNMENT FEES			
	Highest	Lowest	Average
Recording fee	$220	$23	$76
County Tax	$6,750	$22.50	$1,339
TOTAL FEES			
	Highest	Lowest	Average
	$11,395	$1,020	$3,350

- Closing Costs. Figures based on a $125,000 loan amount

> "Nothing happens until something moves."
>
> Albert Einstein

Here is Mr. Einstein again, coming up with the right principle even for money management. Get moving. You now have the knowledge you need.

Get Moving

Do the following within 30 days (or just one of the following):

1) **Do Your Spending Plan.** Know your Income and Outgo.

2) *** Get A Debt Elimination Plan.** Get rid of financial drag. No debt except the mortgage. Get your free debt elimination plan from www.Money-Metrics.com.

3) *** Review Your Mortgage.** Find out if refinancing to a different type of loan will help.

4) **Get Your Credit Report.** Make sure it is correct.

5) *** Get A Home Value Analysis.** Know what your home is worth.

6) *** Get Pre-Approved for a Home Loan.** Know what is possible and where the roadblocks are.

7) **Review Your Insurance Coverage.** Make sure you won't be left financially bust when life happens. Check deductibles and save.

8) **Review Your W-4.** Make sure the right amount is withheld.

9) **Make a Financial Plan.** If you fail to plan, you plan to fail. Timeless quotes can be irritating when they are timelessly true.

* Note: All services with an asterisk are free and available through www.Money-Metrics.com or call 425-373-4045

Basic Principles

Here are some basic principles of money management, or maybe of life and living.

- Live below your means.
- Eliminate credit card debt.
- Have an emergency fund.
- Invest regularly to increase savings and for retirement.
- Build wealth over time.
- Make your money work for you not against you.
- Understand the value of money and learn not to waste it.
- Obtain what you need, not what you want.
- Look for and recognize opportunities to earn extra money or save money instead of spending impulsively.
- Look for opportunities to reduce your state and federal taxes.
- Don't pay someone else to do something you can do yourself.
- Stop paying companies whose sole purpose is to profit from your demise or ignorance.
- Use extra money received (such as taxes, inheritance, bonuses, and gifts) to your benefit by paying off debts or for investments.
- Give back to others and worthy causes.

Fight Parkinson's Laws that state: "A luxury, once enjoyed, becomes a necessity" and "Expenses rise to equal income." It will take energy and commitment to battle these tendencies every day.

You now know more than most people do about money. You can have a more enjoyable life without financial stress. Make the effort and it will pay huge dividends for you down the road. Please contact us if you have questions. It's your money, keep more of it. We look forward to the opportunity to help you.

> "This is priceless. Nobody has ever helped us in such a clear and practical way."
>
> Recent MAP Client

How can you start saving money right now and build for your future. Like all journeys to unfamiliar territory, you will need a good MAP. This MAP is a little different. This MAP is your Money Action Plan. You need to know three things for your MAP to work:

1) Know where you are

2) Know where you want to go

3) Know the best route for you

Where Am I?

To know where you are financially you have to gather current data and information. This includes the following:

- Statement of Financial Position (Assets - Liabilities = Net Worth)

- Income Statement (gross income from all sources)

- Debt Summary (Creditor, Balance, Interest Rate, Minimum Payment)

- Basic and Detailed Spending Plan (Housing, Utilities, Transportation, Food, Clothing, Insurance, Debt, and everything else.)

- Mortgage (Interest Rate, Balance, Payment, more...)

- Homeowners Insurance

- Health Insurance, Supplemental Health Insurance, Health Related Expenses (prescriptions, co-pays, etc), Health Issues

- Life Insurance

- Long Term Care Insurance

- Disability Insurance

- Auto Insurance

- Will, Living Will, Power of Attorney, Estate Planning

- Banking Fees and Costs

- Transportation Costs (Fuel, Parking, Maintenance)

- Cell Phone and Long Distance Costs

- Un-reimbursed Work Expenses

- Education Expenses

- Tax Liabilities

Once you have this information start looking for ways to spend less. Maybe you can increase insurance deductibles or change coverage, use your cell phone less or change to a plan that does not charge for incoming cell calls, find a less expensive place to park for work, refinance to a lower payment mortgage, ways to reduce taxes, and many other possibilities. Once you really know where you spend money, you can start to control it much better.

Where Am I Going?

Goals and objectives, goals and objectives, goals and objectives. Get it yet? Goals and objectives. The usual goal, in the broadest sense, is to save money. Save for what? What do you want? I mean really want. Summer vacations, family trip around he world, family camping trip, college money for the squatters, retirement in Tahiti? What will light you up and help keep you motivated to stay on track. Feel it and believe in it, right down to the ground.

These goals and objectives need to be written down. Be specific as to cost and time frames. Be realistic, be clear, and have both a short-term and long-term approach and then prioritize. Put them in order of importance.

One way to look at this is to use the three buckets of money management discussed earlier.

1) How much do you want for right now. This means the essentials and the lifestyle things you want in your life on a regular basis.

2) What are the things you don't want to happen. These are the things that could be devastating like job loss, major health problems, accidents, and illness. You can pay money to transfer these risks through insurance and emergency funds.

3) What are the things you do want. These are the positive things you want in your life long-term. Travel, college, retirement.

Here is a bad example: "Save for a family vacation to Europe."

This is too vague and undefined.

Here is a better one: "Save $8,500 by 6:23 PM March 27th, 2006 for a 15 day family vacation to Europe that August."

Nice, very specific.

These goals will help keep you on track when it gets difficult and you want to give up or slack off.

What's the best route for me?

Given your unique goals and objectives, what will be the best route to take, the best way to handle your money that will get you to your chosen destination?

In other words, how do you put this into operation day to day? You need to develop a MoP Statement, a Money Policy Statement. This will provide the practical guidelines for how you and your family will handle money on a day-to-day, week-to-week, month-to-month basis.

Your MOPS is your guide, navigator, pilot, rudder, pathfinder... pick an analogy that works for you.

Your MOPS should include:

1) Goals and Objectives (from the previous section).

2) Statements regarding:

- Legitimate uses of the emergency fund.
- The use of credit cards (like – we will not use them).
- What are the basic, essential, and necessary expenses (and their limits). This usually concerns Housing, Utilities, Transportation, Food, Clothing, and Insurance expenses.
- Health insurance needs and expenses.
- Lifestyle spending (recreation, hobbies, dining out, lattes, pizza, drinks, movies, other fun stuff).
- Physical fitness needs and expenses.
- Home maintenance and decorating costs and limits.
- Purchasing used or on sale versus new or full retail (for cars, electronics, furniture, clothing, sporting goods, etc).
- Work objectives and income expectations for the next 5 years.
- How to maximize employment benefits (or self-employment benefits opportunities)
- How you and your spouse (partner) will handle money, pay bills, and review your income and expenses. Who will do what, when, how, etc.
- How often you will review your MAP and MOPS.

The MOPS should give you a set of guidelines that everyone in the family can understand and can live with, given your unique MAP.

You have your MAP, you have your MOPS (hey, and your buckets), now go clean up! Create the life you want.

Too much for you? We help people do this. Visit our website to see examples or give us a call for pricing and more detailed information on creating your personal MAP.

It's your money. Keep more of it.

Web: www.Money-Metrics.com   Office: 425-373-4045

START RIGHT NOW

What can you do right now, today, to start saving money? The following are some ideas on expenses to look at, actions to take, and ideas to ponder to start saving money right now.

Action	Savings/Mo
Talk less on your cell phone.	$25
Spend less on dining out.	$25
Lower insurance premiums: review your insurance policies and increase deductibles (home, auto, all of them).	$30
Buy non-perishable items at discount stores.	$50
Buy basics in bulk and split them with friends.	$25
Do it yourself. (Mow the lawn, paint the house, cleaning, etc)	$25
Think over every purchase over $50.00. Wait at least 24 hours. Comparison shop.	$50
Review your health insurance options and shop for less expensive coverage.	$50
Pack lunches for work and school.	$25
Park in a cheaper spot, further away.	$10
Walk or bike more.	$10
Carpool or take the bus.	$10
Cancel magazine subscriptions.	$5
Cancel the almost never used health club membership.	$20
Lower the thermostat.	$5
Cancel the premium cable TV service.	$20
Cancel the premium telephone services.	$10
TOTAL SAVED/MONTH	**$370**

Note: $370/month invested at 6% for 5 years = $28,814

You can also download the 66 Ways to Save Money from www.Money-Metrics.com.

About Money Metrics

We help people hang on to more of their money.

Most people today feel they work harder, save less, and borrow more. They can't quite figure out where the money goes every month. No matter what their income, occupation, or education most people have never been taught about the basic metrics of money management. We help people get organized, get control, and get moving toward financial success.

Our mission is to make a difference in people's lives through practical financial education delivered with integrity, direct communication, and positive personal support. We do this through the following services:

1) Financial Education - To close the knowledge gap. Learn how to keep more of your money.

2) Money Action Plans - To quickly diagnose and develop solutions to urgent problems and/or create new opportunities.

3) Mortgage Support and Advocacy - To take the fear, frustration, and confusion out of home loans.

4) Financial Coaching and Support - To help you get and stay on a solid financial track.

Money Metrics Workshops are delivered to employees in the workplace, either in groups or through web conferencing. We teach the fundamentals that are represented in this manual and provide other professional resources to attendees via our relationships with real estate agents, financial advisors, insurance agents, CPA's, and other service partners. Call or visit our website at www.Money-Metrics.com to schedule or inquire about a workshop.

For more information visit www.Money-Metrics.com

For questions and comments or to receive other services please contact:

Robert Pessemier
Phone: 425-373-4045
Email: bob@Money-Metrics.com

About the Author

Robert Pessemier is President of Money Metrics, author of *The Money Metrics Manual*, an Accredited Financial Counselor, an Accredited Asset Management Specialist, a Licensed Mortgage Broker in Washington State, provides Money Management and Mortgage Consulting and Money Metrics Workshops to clients around the U.S.

He is also a ten-year veteran of the fire service, was a Firefighter, Lieutenant, and Assistant Fire Marshal, former Washington State Fire Training Academy Instructor, decorated for courage and bravery beyond the call of duty, author of *Up In Smoke: A Business Guide to Fire and Life Safety* which was nominated for a national award from the American Risk & Insurance Association; has been interviewed on local, national, and international radio and television shows, and has recently been published in Fire Chief Magazine.

APPENDIX

Forms and worksheets:

Statement of Financial Position

ASSETS

Cash/Cash Equivalents

Checking Account Balance	
Savings Account Balance	
Money Market Account Balance	
Certificate of Deposit Balance	
Treasury Bill Value	
Savings Bonds Value	
Other Cash Value	
Sub-Total	

Invested Assets

Stocks	
Bonds	
Mutual Funds	
IRA	
Vested Portion of Retirement	
401k	
Other Invested Assets	
Sub-Total	

Daily Use Assets

Home Value	
Vehicles	
Personal Property	
Other Use Assets	
Sub-Total	

TOTAL ASSETS	

Financial Statement - continued

LIABILITIES

Mortgage Balance	
Credit Card Debt	
Vehicle Loan Balances	
Other Debt Balances	
TOTAL LIABILITIES	

Assets - Liabilities =

	NET WORTH

Basic Spending Plan

Item	Amount/Month
HOUSING	
First Mortgage	
2nd/HELOC	
Repairs/Fees	
UTILITIES	
Electricity	
Water	
Gas	
Phone	
Trash	
TRANSPORTATION	
Car Payment 1	
Car Payment 2	
Gas & Oil	
Repairs & Tires	
FOOD	
Groceries	
Dining Out	
CLOTHING	
Adults	
Children	
INSURANCE	
Homeowners	
Health/Medical	
Life & Other	
Car Insurance	
CREDIT CARDS/DEBT	
Total Basic Outgo	
Gross Monthly Income	
Balance	

Credit Cards and Debt

	Creditor	Balance	Rate	Min. Payment
1				
2				
3				
4				
5				
6				
7				
8				
9				
10				
	Total		Total	

Money Metrics

We help people hang on to more of their money.

Most people today feel they work harder, save less, and borrow more. They can't quite figure out where the money goes every month. No matter what their income, occupation, or education most people have never been taught about the basic metrics of money management. We help people get organized, get control, and get moving toward financial success.

Our mission is to make a difference in people's lives through practical financial education delivered with integrity, direct communication, and positive personal support. We do this through the following services:

5) Financial Education - To close the knowledge gap. Learn how to keep more of your money.

6) Money Action Plans - To quickly diagnose and develop solutions to urgent problems and/or create new opportunities.

7) Mortgage Support and Advocacy - To take the fear, frustration, and confusion out of home loans.

8) Financial Coaching and Support - To help you get and stay on a solid financial track.

Money Metrics Workshops are delivered to employees in the workplace, either in groups or through web conferencing. We teach the fundamentals that are represented in this manual and provide other professional resources to attendees via our relationships with real estate agents, financial advisors, insurance agents, CPA's, and other service partners. Call or visit our website at www.Money-Metrics.com to schedule or inquire about a workshop.

For questions and comments? Please contact:

Robert Pessemier
Phone: 425-373-4045
Email: bob@Money-Metrics.com